BROKEN WINGS

CONTENTS

Polish Air Force 1939	4
Dutch and Belgian Air Force 1940	12
French Air Force 1940	16
Royal Air Force 1940	74
Yugoslav Army Air Force & Hellenic Air Force 1941	100
Red Army Air Force 1941	104

Broken Wings
©Canfora Publishing 2019
ISBN: 978-91-984775-4-2
Design: Toni Canfora
Print: Printall, Estonia

Canfora Publishing / Canfora Grafisk Form
Upplandsgatan 96A
113 44 Stockholm, Sweden
www.canfora.se

INTRODUCTION

In just a few months, we will witness the 80th anniversary of the beginning of World War II. Unfortunately, there are few veterans of the Blitzkrieg years who are still with us. However, many of their stories remain, along with a large amount of their photographs. As I write this on Memorial Day, I find myself in awe of the courage of the Allied pilots in those dark days, who often flew into battle with little hope of surviving, to say nothing of succeeding in their mission. Maybe in those awful moments they thought they had lost the war. But in the end, the Blitz was blunted, the Germans turned back, and justice and freedom prevailed. Their sacrifices leave us forever in their debt.

The editor and I decided to use some of those antique photos to tell the story of the Allied air forces that fought against the Blitzkrieg from September of 1939 until the end of 1941. This book is a special collection of photographs, many of them taken by German soldiers during their advance across the European continent. Many of the images come from my own collection, and have never been published before. They provide an interesting look into the details of the air war in the Blitzkrieg era, when very little went well for Allied air forces facing the Luftwaffe.

I suspect that readers of this book will find that some of these unique images raise more questions than they answer. I further suspect that the readers' natural curiosity will lead them to find out more, and probably more than I ever could. I am happy to be the match that lights the fuse for those aviation historians, enthusiasts and modelers. Enjoy the images, and wherever they influence your mind to go.

Tom Laemlein

Resources of the early air war in World War II are not so easy to come by. There are many scattered magazine articles, and small entries in larger works. The following are particularly useful references, and I am grateful to have had them available to me:

Air War For Yugoslavia, Greece and Crete 1940-41
Christopher Shores and Brian Cull with Nicola Malizia
Grub Street 2008
As with all the other volumes in this series, an amazing work.

The Battle of France Then and Now
Six Nations Locked In Aerial Combat September 1939 To June 1940
by Peter D. Cornwell. After The Battle 2007
An outrageous amount of detailed research, day by day, throughout the entirety of the Spring 1940 campaign. Incredible and indispensable.

Curtiss Hawk H-75 in French Service
by Lionel Persyn. STRATUS s.c. 2010
The Hawk H-75 is an extremely important aircraft in the 1940 campaign and this book covers it very well.

French Aircraft From 1939-1942 (2 Volumes)
by Dominique Breffort & Andre Jouineau. Histoire & Collections 2004
Fantastic illustrations and a wealth of information in two tight volumes.

Barbarossa Victims: Luftwaffe Kills In The East
Tomasz J. Kopanski. Mushroom Model Magazine Special 2001
One of the few visual documentations available on the air war over the Eastern Front during 1941. Very well done.

POLISH AIR FORCE 1939

A Bartel BM-5ds observation aircraft captured at Radom. A pair of PWS-26 advanced trainers and a PZL.23 Karas' bomber can be seen in the background.

The distinctive PZL P.7a 999 near the Polish main aircraft depot at Deblin.

FZL.23 Karas' captured while being transported near the town of Lecznz.

PZL.23 Karas' at Radom, inscribed by the Germans "Nach Berlin" (To Berlin).

German recon troops pose with a RWD 8 trainer. This aircraft was also popular in Polish civilian aviation.

PZL P.11 outside Warsaw.

Left:
PZL P.7/11 prototype at Krosno.

Lublin R-VIII bis seaplane at Chalupy, slowly sinking after its floats were damaged.

Two PZL.23 Karas' serve as a dramatic back-drop for these Luftwaffe troops inspecting wrecks at a Polish airfield, November 1939.

PZL P.7a of the 162nd Fighter Group at Lodz.

▽ ⊙ DUTCH AND BELGIAN AIR FORCE 1940

Dutch Fokker DXXII written off at Ypenburg, May 10, 1940. Few of the Dutch fighters survived the fierce Luftwaffe attacks on their fields.

May 10, 1940 was a difficult day for the Belgian Air Force. This Gladiator was hit and burnt out at Schaffen.

One of the Belgian CR.42s, damaged in the attacks on the aerodrome at Mivelles.

Belgian Gladiators caught on the ground at Schaffen.

More than 100 Fairey Fox were still in service with the Belgian Air Force when the Germans attacked. This is one of many that were lost on the ground Mivelles, May 10, 1940.

Right page, bottom left:
Dutch Fokker G1 heavy fighter destroyed at Bergen, May 10, 1940.

Right page, bottom right:
Dutch Fokker D XXI fighter destroyed at Ypenburg airfield on May 10, 1940.

Belgian Gladiators and Hurricanes share a common grave. Much of the Belgian Air Force was wrecked in the first few days of the German attack.

◉ FRENCH AIR FORCE 1940

"Sergent Portain": A French Amiot 143 bomber captured intact as the Wehrmacht surged into France in late May 1940.

German General Rommel was a keen photographer, and he took this image of an abandoned French Amiot 143 bomber as his 7th Panzer Division drove through France to reach the Channel coast on June 10, 1940.

Although the Amiot 143, originally adopted in 1935, was obsolete by the beginning of WWII, nearly 90 of the old bombers were still in service at the time of the German invasion. The Amiot served primarily as night bombers, dropping more than 500 tons of bombs before the Armistice in June. Amiot 143 plodded along at barely 180 mph, but it could carry up to 3,600 pounds of bombs using internal and external racks. Amiot 143 bases as of May 10, 1940 are listed as Montdidier, Roye-Amy, Troyes-Barberey, and Chaumont-Semoutiers.

German officers pose with a Bloch MB 200, captured at Troyes.

Right page, top:
The Bloch MB 200 was adopted in 1935 and had been almost completely phased out of front line service by May 1940 (Bombardment Group 10 at Troyes was mixed with Amiot 143 bombers). The MB 200's bomb load (2,600 lbs) and defensive armament (3x 7.5mm MAC 1934 MGs) was light.

A good view of the nose section of a Bloch MB 200.

The "greenhouse" nose and turret of a Farman 222 bomber.

As of May 10, 1940, the Bloch MB 210 was still flying with three French bomb groups. The MB 210 had proven to be somewhat of a disappointment after its introduction in late 1936. By September 1939, the French were transitioning to newer, more versatile aircraft.

The odd, dome-turret nose of the Bloch MB 210. Nose armament was a single 7.5mm MAC 1934 machine gun.

Broken gear: Bloch MB 210 on one foot.

Right:
The similarly shaped nose and turret of the earlier MB 200.

War trophy: German troops examine a Bloch MB 210. Note the open cockpit door, extending upwards.

The Martin Model 167F entered French service (called Glenn Martin 167 A-3 in France) during early 1940. By May, Martin bombers equipped four combat bomb groups. The Model 167 performed well in combat over France, its high speed (304 mph) and maneuverability made it difficult to intercept. After the armistice, the Martin bombers were evacuated to French North Africa.

German troops examine a Bloch MB 210. Note the RAF Beechcraft Model 17 Traveler in the background.

The French Navy acquired a version of the Chance-Vought SB2U Vindicator dive bomber. Beginning in July 1939, the French began receiving the Vought V-156-F. During the German invasion, the Vought-156-Fs equipped two land-based naval squadrons (AB 1 & AB 3). Heavy losses were suffered as the dive bombers attacked bridgeheads and Panzer columns.

Vought 156-F of French Naval Squadron AB 1, bellied in at Villers-St Christophe after being shot down during an attack on the canal bridges. May 20, 1940.

A tattered Vought 156-F provides a trophy photo for German troops at Le Palyvestre.

French antique: Luftwaffe men pose by a bullet-riddled and tattered Loire et Olivier Leo 20. The LeO 20 bomber was introduced in 1928 and officially retired in 1939.

Vought 156-F of AB 1 crashed at Villers-St Christophe. The French Navy dive-bombers only operated from land during the 1940 fighting, as the carrier "Bearn" was unsuitable for combat operations.

Loire-Nieuport 401 of Naval Squadron AB2 brought down by flak after attacking canal bridges on May 20, 1940.

Left page:
The Bloch MB.131 suffered heavily in both day and night bombing missions during the early months of the war, and by May 1940 the type was limited to one recon group (GR I/55) at Lure. About 140 MB.131 were built and the bombers originally entered service in the summer of 1938. Maximum bomb load was less than 2,000 lbs and overall performance was poor.

The Potez 631 was France's heavy fighter, similar in concept to the German Bf110. Unfortunately, the 631's performance was underwhelming as the fighter was slower than many German bombers in 1940.

Left page, top:
A wrecked Potez 63.11 recon aircraft. The 63.11 suffered the heaviest losses of any French type during the German invasion, with more than 220 lost.

Left page, bottom:
Germans examine a Potez 63.11. With its large greenhouse nose, the Potez was France's most effective tactical recon aircraft.

The Potez 631 fighter featured relatively heavy armament: two 20mm Hispano-Suiza HS.404 cannons and four 7.5mm MAC 1934 machine guns.

Detail views of the Potez 63.11 tactical recon aircraft and light bomber.

In recovery: German troops captured this wrecked Potez 63.11 loaded aboard a trailer. Note the details of the Gnome-Rhone 14N-49 engine and the greenhouse nose.

By the beginning of June 1940, more than 700 Potez 63.11s were delivered to French Air Force combat units. More than 200 of these aircraft were in service with the Vichy Air Force by November 1941.

The Potez 63.11 was not often used as a light bomber or ground attack aircraft, but when it was the losses were heavy. Normal frontal armament was three 7.5mm MAC machine guns in a pod beneath the nose. Sometimes an additional four 7,5mm MGs were added beneath the wings for strafing attacks.

Right page, bottom left:
A captured Dewoitine D.510 inspected by Waffen SS troops.

Right page, bottom right:
While their columns push ever forward in the distance, German troops examine a Potez 63.11 force-landed in a French field.

Germans pose aboard a wrecked Bloch MB 174, France's most effective recon aircraft of the 1940 campaign.

Strange circumstances. A Potez 63.11 on a French street corner.

German motorcyclists, wearing their rubberized protective gear, examine a Potez 631. The French heavy fighter proved ineffective as an interceptor, and began to be used in the ground attack role. Many fell victim to German flak and fighters.

When first introduced during 1936 the Dewoitine D.510 was the most advanced fighter in the world. By the spring of 1940 it was an antique. However, when war broke out in September 1939, almost 150 MB.510s were still in front line service. By May 10, 1940 only a handful remained, handling patrols in quiet sectors.

General Erwin Rommel photographed these Morane Saulnier M.S. 406 fighters during the 7th Panzer Division's drive through France.

Right page, top:
Morane Saulnier M.S. 406 fighters found at Cambrai field.

Another photo taken by Rommel of captured M.S 406 fighters.

M.S. 406 shot down and stripped by German souvenir hunters.

At the beginning of WWII, the maneuverable and strong Morane Saulnier M.S. 406 was highly competitive with German fighters. By May of 1940, and the arrival of the Bf109E in great numbers, the M.S. 406 had become obsolete. Even so, the Moranes recorded 190 kills during May-June 1940 against 150 of their own shot down. Almost half of all French pilots killed in the German invasion were flying the M.S. 406.

While the Dewoitine D.520 was among the most modern of the French fighters (entering service in January 1940), it was considered rather difficult to fly. Even so, it performed well enough in combat, with D.520 pilots claiming 114 kills before the Armistice, against 85 losses.

M.S. 406 nosed over. By the Armistice, more than 300 Moranes had been lost due to all causes.

Several Morane Saulnier M.S. 406 were captured intact at Cambrai.

M.S. 406 stripped by souvenir hunters. This wreck was one of many found at Cambrai.

More M.S. 406's stripped by German souvenir hunters.

Details of the M.S. 406's Hispano-Suiza 12Y-31 V12 engine. The Morane's top speed was 300 mph.

Tactical recon wrecks: An ANF-Les Mureaux 117 (foreground) and a Potez 39 beside it. Note the MS 406 fighters in the background.

Dewoitine D.520 fighters were relatively close to the German Bf109E in performance: the French aircraft was slower but more maneuverable. The D.520's armament was lighter, with 4x 7.5mm MAC machine guns in the wings and a engine-mounted 20mm Hispano-Suiza HS.404 cannon. The Germans used some for training while sending many to Bulgaria and Italy for operational service.

M.S. 406 disarmed: A Morane fighter awaits its fate as the Germans take over. All of this aircraft's armament has been removed, from the engine-mounted 20mm Hispano-Suiza HS.404 cannon and the 7.5mm MAC 1934 machine guns in each wing.

The fall of France: The arrogant pose of the German atop this tattered and abandoned Morane Saulnier M.S. 406 speaks volumes about the bitter end of hostilities brought on by the French Armistice of June 22, 1940.

Arsenal VG 33 fighters captured while in the final stages of production.

German troops examine a group of Caudron CR.714 fighters. These small and fragile fighters were flown heroically by the collection of Polish pilots who had escaped to France.

Breguet Bre. 693 fighter-bomber shot down and burnt out after being hit by German flak.

Grounded Hawk: The Curtiss Hawk H-75A3 of S/Lt Rey (flying with GC 1/5), brought down by German fighters on May 18, 1940. French Hawk pilots claimed 230 kills for a loss of just 29 of their own during the Spring 1940 campaign.

Curtiss H-75A3 wrecked during a bombing raid and subsequently stripped for parts.

Blitzkrieg detritus: captured Hawk 75s crowded in with Breguet Bre. 693s.

Curtiss H-75A1 brought down in late May 1940.

Curtiss H-75 GC II/4, flown by Adj Jean Paulhan, brought down by Bf109s on June 9, 1940.

Left:
Captured Curtiss H-75s photographed by General Rommel.

Interesting view of the wing armament of a shattered Curtiss H-75A3. The French equipped these aircraft with two license-built FN-Browning MGs in each wing, and two more mounted atop the cowling.

German trophy photo showing the gun ports in the cowling for two 7.5mm MGs of a Curtiss H-75A1.

Curtiss Hawk H-75A3 flown by S/Lt Rey of GC 1/5, shot down on May 18, 1940.

A Curtiss H-75A1 displayed along with other captured French equipment at Missy-sur-Aisne during the summer of 1940. In the foreground is the famous French Canon de 75mm Modele 1897. In the background to the right are Canon de 155mm Long Mle M1917 Schneider guns.

Right page, top right:
Bloch MB 152: A derelict Bloch MB.152, hastily camouflaged by the French and then captured before it could be repaired.

Right page, bottom right:
SS men examine a Bloch MB 152. Note the MS 406 in the background.

Curtiss H-75 on display at Missy-sur-Aisne. The Hawk was originally brought down on June 6, 1940 with S/C Josef Janeba of GC II/5 at the controls.

Probably the most photographed Curtiss Hawk of the 1940 campaign. Beneath its nose is a French 47mm APX anti-tank gun. To the right is a 8mm Hotchkiss M1914 machine gun. Farther right is a Brandt mle 27 81mm mortar. Missy-sur-Aisne, summer 1940.

Bizarre German snapshot of a Bloch MB.152 crashed into the side of a French house. The German troops in the foreground appear to have an interesting war story to tell.

The Bloch MB.152 was a relatively sturdy fighter, capable of withstanding considerable damage. Nevertheless, approximately ninety of the Bloch fighters were lost during May and June of 1940.

Approximately 35 of the Bloch MB.155 variant were built, which were powered by the Gnome-Rhone 14N-49 engine. Armament and performance remained the same as the MB.152.

France's long winter begins: German troops assemble on a snow-covered Bloch MB.152 for a trophy photo in early 1941.

Left page:
Despite its reputation for sturdiness, the Bloch MB.152 was handicapped by poor performance, predominately its lack of maneuverability and short range.

A captured Breguet Bre. 693 ground attack fighter-bomber. One of the more modern French designs in the spring of 1940, the Bre .693s were not ready for service until March 1940.

Left page:
The Bloch MB.152 featured relatively heavy armament for a single-seat fighter in 1940 with 2x 20mm cannons and 2x 7.5mm MGs. The wing-mounted Hispano-Suiza HS.404 cannons fired an effective explosive shell at a rate of about 11 rounds per second. Unfortunately the HS.404 was only fed by drum magazines, which had some jamming issues and contained just 60 rounds of ammunition.

Breguet Bre. 693s suffered heavily from German light flak (20mm & 37mm) brought forward to cover the advancing Panzer columns.

Engine reliability and undercarriage failures also dogged the Breguet Bre. 693 ground attack aircraft. The Bre. 693 was powered by two Gnome-Rhone 14M radial engines. Maximum speed was 304 mph.

Breguet Bre. 693's armament consisted of 2x 7.5mm MAC 1934 machine guns and 20mm Hispano-Suiza HS.404 cannon firing forward. A 7.5mm MG covered the dorsal and ventral positions. Bomb load was 1,000 lbs.

Detailed view of the Breguet Bre. 693. Note the gun port for the 20mm Hispano-Suiza HS.404 cannon in the lower fuselage. In the nose you can see the weapons bay for the two 7.5mm MAC machine guns.

By the time the Armistice was signed, 119 Breguet 693s were destroyed or written off, equating to an operational loss rate of 63%. Nearly 50% of the Breguet crews were casualties.

Breguet 270 recon aircraft shot down. Wheel spats have been removed to prevent the wheels becoming clogged with mud.

A DeHavilland Tiger Moth trainer sits among the detritus of defeat. French 155mm GPF cannons can be seen in background of this hodge-podge collection point of captured equipment.

Right page, bottom:
The Breguet 270 equipped three observation groups at the beginning of the war, and were still in service in several tactical recon groups on May 10, 1940. Operational losses for the type were heavy.

Nose dive: Potez 25 crashed head first.

The odd Breguet 270 "sesquiplane" observation aircraft.

71

German officers examine a Potez 25. Introduced in 1925, the Potez 25 was still serving in small numbers with tactical recon groups when Germany invaded. Note the bomb racks on this aircraft. Maximum bomb load for the Potez 25 was 440 lbs.

German motorcyclists pause by a Morane-Saulnier MS.315. The parasol-wing MS.315 was introduced in 1932 as a primary trainer.

⊙ ROYAL AIR FORCE 1940

Hurricane nosed over and abandoned on a French field. Note the long-range fuel tanks beneath the wings.

Left page:
Hawker Hurricanes provided the fighter component of the RAF Advanced Air Striking Force in France. In total, 452 Hurricanes were sent to the Continent before the withdrawal of British forces. Only 66 returned to England.

Grounded and stripped of anything useful, yet this Hurricane's pilot seat remains.

The majority of the Hurricane's exterior surfaces were linen-fabric, and in this case they were totally consumed by the fire.

The best of the Allied fighters in the spring of 1940. Hurricanes scored the first RAF victory of the war, downing four He 115s on October 2, 1939. During the French campaign, Hurricane pilots recorded 300 kills between May 10 and May 21, 1940. Nearly 390 Hurricanes were lost to enemy action or abandoned during that time.

Left page, bottom left:
German cavalrymen pick over a downed Hurricane for souvenirs.

Left page, bottom right:
Balkan interlude: Hurricane abandoned at Athens, Greece. May 1941.

Ten Hurricane squadrons met the full force of the German Blitzkrieg in Western Europe. This one fell victim to Luftwaffe fighters. It is equipped with a new Rotol constant-speed propeller (this example made of wood), which helped increase the Hurricane's performance and made it more competitive against German fighters.

Left page, top:
Hurricane stripped to the bone. Note the Rolls Royce Merlin engine and the empty wing bays for the four .303 caliber Browning machine guns.

Left page, bottom:
German troops clown near a completely burnt out Hurricane. Note the man holding the small bomb in the foreground.

An abandoned Hurricane victimized by German souvenir hunters.

Right page, top:
Hurricane wrecks left at Abbeville after the British withdrawal from France.

Right page, bottom:
A burnt out Hurricane provides a curiosity for German cyclists.

To the victors go the spoils: German trophy photos of Hurricane wrecks, among the 178 examples of the Hawker fighter left behind in France, destroyed in bombing raids or burned by the British themselves when the aircraft could not be flown out.

By May 21, Hurricanes that could not be flown out were stripped of anything useful and then burned. This was repeated at multiple airfields, and particularly at Abbeville, Lille and Merville.

Left page and above:
A burnt out Hurricane stands as a mute reminder of air battles lost, and those yet to come. "What General Weygand called he Battle of France is over. I expect that the Battle of Britain is about to begin. Upon this battle depends the survival of Christian civilization." Winston Churchill, June 18, 1940.

The Spitfire of Pilot Officer Kenneth Hart of No. 65 Squadron belly-landed on Dunkirk beach after it was damaged in air-to-air combat. P/O Hart set fire to his Spitfire and joined with the troops awaiting evacuation by sea.

Right page, top:
The RAF kept its Spitfires based in England during 1940, but a few examples still fell into German hands. This Spitfire MkIA force landed near Cherbourg on August 15, 1940. It was tested by the Luftwaffe at Rechlin and by German fighter units based in France.

Right page, bottom:
A rarity left behind: a Fleet Air Arm Fairey Seal recon aircraft abandoned in France.

The RAF's Fairey Battle squadrons suffered badly in the air battle over France (13 were lost on the first day of campaign alone). The Battle was essentially obsolete before the start of WWII, and its lack of armor and self-sealing fuel tanks was a deadly handicap by May of 1940. In just six weeks of combat, nearly 200 had been lost in combat.

Right page, top:
Fairey Battle (P2200) of 105 Squadron shot down by flak on May 10, 1940, the first day of the German attack. After belly-landing near Clemency, the crew was taken prisoner.

Right page, bottom:
Fairey Battle written off and left to its fate in France.

Blenheim IV abandoned in the Balkans during the spring of 1941.

Right page, top:
Blenheim wrecks in France. In the foreground, Blenheim "L9243" of 57 Squadron, crashed on landing and was written off at Rouen on May 23, 1940.

Right page, bottom:
A Blenheim boneyard in Greece, April 1941.

German troops pick over an abandoned Blenheim IV for souvenirs. Athens, Greece, April 1941.

Right page, bottom left:
A Short S.25 Sunderland flying boat abandoned in the Mediterranean. These massive aircraft did yeoman work in the evacuation of Crete.

Right page, bottom right:
Another view of the abandoned Sunderland. Note the details of the fuselage and the wing root.

Nearly intact: A Blenheim IV captured in Greece during April 1941. Note the details of the wing construction.

A photo for the folks back home: Luftwaffe men pose atop a Blenheim IV bomber captured in Greece during April 1941.

Left page, top:
Blenheim IV abandoned in France, June 1940.

Left page, bottom:
Blenheim Mk I abandoned at Athens aerodrome in April 1941.

Reach the beach: A Blenheim IV rescued from the Channel surf by the Germans and pulled onto the French shore.

German troops examine an abandoned Westland Lysander. The Lysander debuted in France during the Blitzkrieg as a spotting aircraft and light bomber, as five squadrons flew with the RAF component of the BEF's Army Cooperation Wing. Losses were heavy, with 118 Lysanders destroyed out of the 175 deployed to France.

This abandoned Lysander shows some of its teeth: a .303 caliber Vickers "K" gun for the observer. Two .303 Browning guns could be fitted in the wheel fairings, and up to 500 lbs of small bombs could be carried on the stub wings.

Hitting back: in late 1941, the RAF began its campaign of "leaning over the Channel" and striking German installations in occupied France. These RAF Boston III bombers were brought down in those early missions to reverse the momentum of the Blitzkrieg and begin the liberation of Europe.

Note the blister added to accommodate a Browning machine gun on each side of the nose.

⊕ YUGOSLAV ARMY AIR FORCE &
⊙ HELLENIC AIR FORCE 1941

An attempt at modernization: In 1939, Yugoslavia acquired about a dozen Caproni Ca.311 recon/bombers from Italy.

Left page:
The Yugoslavs purchased a hundred Breguet 19 recon/bombers from France during the 1920s, and then acquired a license to manufacture several hundred of the aircraft (equipping them with a number of different engines). Many were still in service at the time of the German attack in April 1941.

Zmaj Fazir FN trainer/utility aircraft set ablaze by a German attack on their home field. The Fazir FN was simple and sturdy, and was later used by the Italians and the Croatians after Yugoslavia fell.

Wrecked Gloster Mars biplanes of the Hellenic Air Force in 1941. These biplane fighters started out as the Nieuport Nighthawk. When Nieuport closed operations in 1920, Gloster bought the rights to the aircraft, upgraded the engine and produced it as the "Mars". These fighters remained in Greek service until retired from front-line duties in 1938. Note the Junkers G24 in the background.

★ RED ARMY AIR FORCE 1941

I-153 found in Lithuania during early July, 1941. The tail is likely painted with a blue tip.

The wings snapped over on this I-15bis when it crashed during the initial stages of Operation Barbarossa.

Polikarpov I-153 cowling, housing the 800 horsepower Shvetsov M-62 radial engine. Note the fairings for the four 7.62×54mmR ShKAS machine guns, and the launch rails for RS-82 rockets beneath the wings.

I-153 inverted. This aircraft is painted in an overall light grey.

The radio antenna on the top right wing denotes this I-153 as a squadron commander's aircraft.

Blitzkrieg detritus: I-153s mixed among various other Red Air Force types, including an I-16 (rear).

Wehrmacht troops pose with a derelict I-15. Trophy photos like this were commonplace among Germans sorting through the piles of captured Soviet equipment.

Polikarpov I-15 & I-153s in varying states of distress. The stars found on Red Army Air Force aircraft were highly prized by German troops and they were stripped off at the first opportunity.

I-153 stripped by souvenir hunters down to its skeleton.

Put out to pasture: I-153 in a natural "revetment".

Broken wings: tattered I-153. Note the details of the Shvetsov M-62 radial engine.

Right page, top row:
I-153 captured by an SS cavalry unit.

I-153 on a Lithuanian field. Note the cut-out Soviet star.

A mixed bag of Soviet fighters captured, I-153s and an I-16, featuring a wide range of paint schemes.

I-153 captured at Wilno (Vilnius, Lithuania). An R-5 (P-5 light transport variant) is seen in the background.

The airfield at Wilno overflowed with captured Soviet aircraft, I-153s reside with Polikarpov 1-16, and R-5 and U-2 liaison aircraft in the background.

Finnish troops captured this intact Polikarpov I-153 during the late summer of 1941 during the "Continuation War". Note the use of bomb racks as well as the prewar Soviet star, featuring a black circle in the center.

Two more shots of the same aircraft. It seems to have been hastily camouflaged with branches from a birch tree.

"Ishak" (donkey) Polikarpov 1-16 Type 5 fitted with the Shvetsov M-25 engine. Of all Soviet aircraft in service during the initial stages of Operation Barbarossa, the I-16 represented more than 25% of that total. I-16 was more maneuverable than the Bf109E, although clearly inferior in terms of speed, climb, and armament. This aircraft is missing the ShKAS 7.62mm machine gun from its starboard wing mount.

The enclosed canopy of the I-16 Type 5 offered very poor visibility, and was often removed by Soviet pilots. Armament of the Type 5 was sorely limited, with just one ShKAS 7.62mm MG (with 450 rounds per gun) in each wing. A MiG-3 is seen in the background. The tail tip is likely blue. Mitau, Latvia.

Introduced in 1934, the I-16 was the world's first low-wing, monoplane fighter. In 1941, it was still marginally competitive, but only due to its extreme horizontal maneuverability.

A snapshot for the folks back home: German troops clowning with a wrecked I-16 in the winter of 1942.

Russian kids examine an I-16, curiously dumped by the roadside (see also page 126)

I-16 featuring exotic camouflage and the Soviet pilot's badge displayed on the tail.

A German column passes a wrecked I-16. During the first few weeks of Operation Barbarossa, more than 700 of the little Polikarpov fighters had been lost.

Wingless I-16 abandoned along the long road of retreat in the summer of 1941. Note the details of the two 7.62 ShKAS machine guns on the top of the cowling. The ShKAS featured an extremely high rate of fire at 1,800 rounds per minute (30 rounds per second).

I-16 Type 29, towed into captivity by the Wehrmacht. Note the opening in the bottom of the cowling for the 12.7mm UBS machine gun.

A rarely photographed UTI-4 trainer, placed on wooden supports.

A nice side view of an I-16 Type 5 in a seemingly intact condition. The original canopy is still mounted.

A wrecked I-16 Type 17, showing details of its wing-mounted 20mm ShVAK cannon. Two 7.62mm ShKAS machine guns were mounted in the nose.

Wehrmacht troops look over a badly damaged I-16. This photo offers a good view of the frame work behind the pilot's seat.

Strange circumstances: as a convoy passes into the vast expanse of the Eastern Front, Wehrmacht men seem rather amused by this I-16 Type 29's odd final resting place.

UTI-4 (the trainer version of the I-16) captured by the Finns during the early stages of the Continuation War. Nearly 3,200 of these trainers were built between 1938 and 1942. *(Via SA-Kuva)*

I-16 downed during the Soviet Winter War with Finland. Even in the extreme cold, Soviet pilots preferred to fly the I-16 with an open cockpit. *(Via SA-Kuva)*

The same I-16, viewed from underneath. Note the launch rails for the RS-132 rocket (132mm, 2-lbs warhead). *(Via SA-Kuva)*

At the beginning of Operation Barbarossa there were more than 1,000 MiG-3 fighters available to the Red Army Air Force. Unfortunately there were less than 500 pilots trained on the type. Many were wrecked or abandoned in the early days of the invasion.

Left page:
A rare look into the Mikoyan-Gurevich MiG-3. Note the details of the padded pilot's seat, and the tightly packed armament in the nose (2x7.62mm ShKAS and 1x12.7 Berezin UBS).

An iconic image of the Blitzkrieg: a Wehrmacht soldier examines an abandoned MiG-3 while Russia burns in the background.

Left page:
MiG-3 fighters brought down by the Luftwaffe during the invasion of the Soviet Union, summer 1941. Note the details of the Mikulin AM-35A liquid-cooled V12 engine (1,350 HP).

The MiG-3 was never able to perform to its full potential. Its good performance at higher altitudes was rarely of value in the low-altitude air war of the Eastern Front. Weak armament and poor visibility for the pilot also handicapped one of war's more exotic fighters.

Left page:
The MiG-3 had an unusual armament arrangement, with all three machine guns (two 7.62mm ShKAS and a 12.7 Berezin UBS) mounted in the engine cowling. The unique engine cover and gun ports can be seen here.

Petlyakov Pe-2: the initial, horrible losses of the summer of 1941 obscured the achievements of several very capable Soviet aircraft. One of these was the Pe-2 bomber, demonstrating surprising speed, toughness and adaptability.

Left page, top:
Belly landing: Waffen SS soldier looks over a MiG-3 brought down during Operation Barbarossa.

Left page, bottom:
LaGG-3 captured in the winter of 1941-42. Note the launch rails for RS-82 rockets. The LaGG-3 was widely disliked by Soviet pilots.

Luftwaffe men look over the wreck of a Pe-2. Note the details on the Klimov M-105PF V12 engine.

Caught by Luftwaffe fighters, this Pe-2 crashed and burnt out.

Yakovlev Yak-4 light bomber. A slight upgrade over the Yak-2, the Yak-4 was a fast bomber (330 mph) but with a small bomb load (1,300 lbs). Less than 100 were built.

The Yakovlev Yak-2 recon/light bomber. Soviet records indicate that about 70 Yak-2s were in service at the beginning of the German invasion, and that almost all of them were lost by the end of the summer.

A Beriev MBR-2 flying boat captured by the Finns during the Winter War. *(Via SA-Kuva)*

Left page, top:
German trophy hunters pick over a crashed Pe-2.

Left page, bottom:
A tattered Polikarpov R-5 equipped with skis. First introduced in 1930, the R-5 served the Red Army Air Force as a light bomber, recon, trainer and liaison aircraft until early 1944.

The R-5 was commonly found on Soviet fields during the early stages of Operation Barbarossa.

R-5s on a bombed and cratered Soviet field.

Polikarpov U-2 "Kukuruznik" ("Crop Duster"). More than 30,000 of these simple but sturdy aircraft were built by the Soviets.

A good view of the R-5 cockpit. Note that the Soviet star has not yet been cut out by souvenir hunters.

The Soviet UT-1 trainer: most of these aircraft were painted in an overall light silver with bright red highlights.

A very rare U-2SS ambulance aircraft.

Polikarpov U-2 captured in the summer of 1941.

Beginning in late 1941, the hard-working U-2 would become known as the Po-2, adding night harassment bombing to its resume. A Stalinetz tractor is seen in the foreground.

Wehrmacht men are putting a significant weight to the landing gear when posing for a trophy photo aboard this R-5.

A sharp close-up view of the Shvetsov M11D 5-cylinder engine (125 HP) of the U-2.

Several of the massive, but archaic Tupelov TB-3 bombers were still flying in 1941. This is a good view of its Mikulin M17F V12 engines.

Right page:
The Tupelov TB-3 was officially retired in 1939, but the Red Army Air Force still had more than 500 in service at the beginning of the German invasion. Even by August 1941, the TB-3 still represented 25% of the Soviet bomber force. It was a popular backdrop for many German trophy photos during Barbarossa.

TB-3s were also active during the Winter War with Finland. This one is thoroughly inspected after being captured by the Finns. *(Via SA-Kuva)*

Right page, top:
A front view of the same aircraft.

Right page, bottom:
TB-3s were active in the night-bomber role until 1943. It was a massive aircraft, with 137-foot wingspan and weighing almost 38,000 lbs when loaded.

Tupelov ANT-6A (Soviet polar research aviation variant of the TB-3) captured during the German invasion of 1941.

The Tupelov SB high speed bomber made up more than 90% of the Soviet bomber force in 1941. Many hundreds of the SB bombers were destroyed in the early days of the German offensive.

SB-2M-100A captured intact on a field overrun by the Germans. Summer 1941. A Kfz. 15 Horch command car is seen in the background.

Left page:
SB-2s brought down during the summer of 1941. Note the very random and crude camouflage scheme.

Detail of the SB-2 rear gun position of the aircraft from page 151, armed with a ShKAS 7.62mm machine gun.

Left page, top:
SB-2 light bomber, showing its nose armament of twin 7.62mm ShKAS machine guns.

Left page, bottom :
A rare shot of the USB dual-control trainer version of the SB-2.

German troops posing with a recently captured SB-2.

Another view of a USB dual-control trainer. The instructor sat in the open cockpit.

This photo offers a detailed view of the pilot's position of the SB-2 as well as the raised rivets of the airframe.

Left page, top:
SB-2 badly damaged, probably by a German SD-2 (2 kg) "butterfly bomb".

Left page, bottom:
The wreck of a USB trainer. Note the details of the wing construction.

Interesting image of a partially stripped IL-2 examined by German troops. Curiously, RS-82 rockets are still attached to their launch rails beneath the wing.

Left page, top:
The famed Ilyushin IL-2 Sturmovik was available in small numbers (more than 200 at the front during June 1941) from the early days of the German invasion. Here, German troops examine the wing-mounted VYa-23 23mm cannon.

Left page, bottom:
IL-2 wrecked by German air attack. Note the details of the 23mm wing cannon and the launching rails for RS-82 rockets.

An IL-2 wreck deposited in town provides a curiosity for German troops and a playground for local kids.

Wing of an IL-2 blasted from the sky. Initial losses of the Sturmovik were heavy until better tactics were worked out. Note the details on the RS-82 rocket launching rails.

Crashed and burnt out IL-2. In the dark days of 1941 and early 1942, IL-2s were often used as a substitute fighter aircraft, with mixed results.

IL-2 trophy photo for a happy Wehrmacht soldier in the pilot's seat. This aircraft has 20mm ShVAK cannons in its wings. Note the I-16 in the background.

Despite its inauspicious debut during Operation Barbarossa, the IL-2 Sturmovik would become one of the most famous attack aircraft of all time, as well as the most produced military aircraft in history.

Ilyushin DB-3F (designated IL-4 in March 1942). The most numerous Soviet medium bomber of the war, DB-3s bombed Berlin as early as August 8, 1941. Early armament consisted of 7.62mm ShKAS MGs in the nose, ventral and dorsal turret positions. Later, the turret weapon was upgraded to a 12.mm UBT machine gun.

A DB-3M wrecked during a German bombing raid.

Belly-landed DB-3F. Note the details of the wing construction and the Tumansky M-88B 14 cylinder engine.

Good rear view of the DB-3F, showing off the bulbous rear turret. At the time, the DB-3 was the most expensive aircraft in the Red Army Air Force, owing to its modern design and all-metal construction.

Left page, bottom:
An abandoned DB-3F. It appears that some effort was made to camouflage the bomber while it awaited repair.

An early production DB-3 with a badly damaged nose. This aircraft is painted overall silver and was captured near Pskov in the late summer of 1941.

Left page, top:
German troops clown around atop a burnt-out DB-3F.

Left page, bottom :
Sharing space with a I-153 and several Luftwaffe aircraft, this DB-3F is seen at the end of June 1941 at Borisov field (Belarus).

Sukhoi Su-2 light bomber brought down by German anti-aircraft fire. With more than 200 Su-2s destroyed in combat by early 1942, the aircraft was withdrawn from front-line service.

Left page, top:
Snowbound: Wrecked Sukhoi Su-2 photographed after the first snows of late 1941.

Left page, bottom:
Wehrmacht column passes by a shot-down Su-2 light bomber. Many Su-2s were lost in ground attack operations during the initial phases of the German invasion.

The Su-2 proved vulnerable to both Luftwaffe fighters and Wehrmacht AA fire.

Su-2 carried four 7.62mm ShKAS machine guns in the wings, along with a ShKAS in the dorsal turret and one in a belly hatch position. Bomb load was up to 1,300 pounds or eight RS-82 rockets.

German troops look over an engine-less KhAI-5. The portly Kharkiv design was obsolete well before the war with Germany began.

Left page, bottom left:
Rare bird: The Kharkiv KhAI-5 recon/light bomber.

Left page, bottom right :
A side vew of the same KhAI-5 as above.

The Su-2 proved to be an average design that tended to under-perform in combat.

Left page, bottom left:
A Kharkiv KhAI-5 (see also p.172, bottom left) captured relatively intact in the summer of 1941. The aircraft is overall light silver. These aircraft were encountered in small numbers until the end of 1942.

Left page, bottom right:
Captured SU-2 and DB-3F bombers in the late summer of 1941. Note the I-16 wreck under the DB-3's nose.

Luftwaffe men examine a Sukhoi Su-2. Note the details of the rear gunner's position.